Original title:
Life Is a Journey… But I Forgot the Map

Copyright © 2025 Creative Arts Management OÜ
All rights reserved.

Author: Rory Fitzgerald
ISBN HARDBACK: 978-1-80566-062-0
ISBN PAPERBACK: 978-1-80566-357-7

The Road Less Taken

I took a path, a twisty route,
With squirrels laughing, I gave a shout.
No GPS, just my instincts wild,
Found a hot dog stand—oh, I smiled!

Potholes jumping, like dance routines,
Led me to places where no one's been.
A sign read 'Detour,' I shrugged my fate,
Maybe I'll get somewhere at eight... or late!

Steps into the Abyss

I stepped outside to find my way,
But tripped on the cat—now I'll delay.
Around the corner, a dance group swayed,
Join in the fun? My inner child paid!

Each step a mystery, shoes untied,
Waltzing to nowhere, I tried to glide.
Fell into a puddle, splashed like a king,
Next time, I swear, I'll stick to the bling!

Echoes of Forgotten Trails

The echoes call of paths once made,
But in this maze, I'm slightly swayed.
I found a map—but it was a menu,
A place for tacos, that'll do, that'll do!

With every corner, a new delight,
Ice cream spills in the sun—what a sight!
Murmurs of laughter, the trees join in,
At least this adventure has free ice cream!

Footprints on a Blank Canvas

I wandered out with shoes so bright,
But walked on clouds, what a silly sight!
Each step a splash of colors new,
Paint me a rainbow, can I join you?

With every footfall, I made a mark,
Got lost in the park—no dogs to bark.
So I just twirled on a soft green lawn,
No map in hand, just my silly dawn!

Quest for the Untold

In a land where socks go missing,
I lost my way, but kept on wishing.
With every turn, a new surprise,
A dance with fate beneath the skies.

A bird once told me, 'Just relax!'
Yet here I stand, with no true tracks.
I chased my shadow, tried to flee,
To find out where the next wrong's be.

The Compass of Curiosity

My compass spins, a wild flirt,
Points to the garden, or maybe the dirt.
I followed a bee, it led me astray,
Buzzing with laughter; what a silly display!

With maps that crumple in the rain,
I laugh at the mud that stains my brain.
A treasure hunt for lost car keys,
I declare the bushes as my expertise!

Meandering Through Memory

I wandered past the old ice cream stand,
And laughed at the thought of it all unplanned.
Each scoop a memory, dripped down my hand,
Chocolate or chaos? Ah, life is just grand!

I took a left where I meant to go right,
Found a parade of cats, a hilarious sight.
They led me to nowhere but laughter's embrace,
In this meandering journey, I found my own place.

Maps of the Heart

I drew a map with crayons bright,
To find love's treasure, what a silly plight!
But every 'X' just led to more fun,
A dance in the rain, oh, how time had run!

With every wrong turn, a giggle or two,
I found hidden gems where wildflowers grew.
A heart full of joy, with no need to steer,
In the chaos of maps, my path is so clear!

The Path Beneath My Feet

I set out on a sunny day,
With a coffee and a grin, hooray!
But left my compass at the bar,
Now I wander like a lost celeb star.

Each twist and turn, I just go round,
Chasing shadows, lost, confound.
The geese are laughing, can't you see?
Mapless, I make my own mystery!

Roads Untraveled

I took a road less traveled by,
Thought I'd soar, instead I fly.
Turn left, right, oh what a game,
Just hoping I won't end up in the same.

A squirrel waved as I passed by,
Was that a clue, or just a lie?
With every step a new surprise,
Wait, was that my shoe? Oh my, oh my!

Navigating the Unseen

I packed my map, or so I thought,
But then it vanished, oh what a plot!
Now I'm relying on Google's vibe,
Yet every turn leads to a tribe!

They dance and sing, what a sight!
"Join us!" they shout, "It feels so right!"
I wander off, lost in the fray,
But they won't let me go, hip hip hooray!

Steps in the Mist

I walked into the morning mist,
Whispers of paths I hope exist.
Yet all I find is friendly fog,
And a cat that looks like a dialogue!

With every step, I twist and twine,
Hoping I'll find a sunny line.
But alas, I trip, then tumble down,
At least I get laughs from the whole town!

Beyond the Familiar Horizon

In pockets deep, I find my snacks,
Bright sun above, no moving tracks.
The compass spins, a funny fate,
I wander off, oh, isn't this great?

With squirrels chattering, I make my way,
Chasing shadows that lead astray.
Maps are for clever folks, it seems,
I prefer to frolic in wildest dreams.

A sandwich here, some chips to share,
Oops! I tripped on a random chair.
The world is big, and I just roam,
Why look for roads when I have home?

Each twist and turn, a path I must write,
Finding new wonders, what pure delight!
With laughter loud, I'll dance and sing,
Forget the maps, let adventure bring.

Trails Teeming with Dreams

With mismatched socks, I tread so bold,
The trail's not marked, or so I'm told.
My buddy laughs, oh what a surprise,
We're lost again! Just look at those skies!

A frog on a log sings sweet disdain,
"Where's your map?" But I feel no pain.
The wildflowers giggle as I step by,
"Who needs directions? Just give it a try!"

I spot a squirrel, it looks quite wise,
But I bet he'd point with mischievous eyes.
"Keep going straight, or maybe left!"
I flip a coin, a journey bereft.

With mud on my shoes and sun on my face,
This unplanned route finds its own pace.
I embrace the chaos, let spontaneity flow,
In trails teeming with dreams, I steal the show.

The Shape of Lost Things

Round and round, like my old lost phone,
In shadows of trees, hilariously alone.
A hat in a puddle, what a fine sight,
Is that a landmark? Oh, not quite right!

My backpack's full of snacks and fears,
Wandering into the great unknown cheers.
A deer raises a brow, does it feel my plight?
"Ever consider staying in a straight flight?"

Rocks that look like beasts of yore,
No, that's just my imagination's lore.
I map out my thoughts in clouds overhead,
"Adventure awaits!" my inner voice said.

With every step, my giggles break free,
Lost in the shape of things I can't see.
I dance with the clouds, my feet in the air,
Who needs a map when you're light as a spare?

Gaze of the Lost Explorer

With my trusty hat, the world in view,
I squint through the trees - is that a clue?
An explorer's gaze, mischief on deck,
Why follow paths? I'll just bounce back!

Whoa! A sign? Oh wait, it's a tree,
Masked as directions, confusing to me.
I spin around, feeling oh-so-sly,
Inviting the sun to my playful sky.

A chirpy bird sings tales of delight,
"Forget your path, just find your flight!"
My heart's the map; it's trusty and true,
With giggles and joy, I'll wander anew.

So here's to mishaps and jolly reprieve,
Unraveled adventures I just can't conceive.
With laughter galore, let the world whirl free,
For every lost moment is magic to me.

Driftwood on the River of Time

I set sail in a boat of dreams,
With snacks and a steering wheel that screams.
The oars I forgot, but it's fine you see,
Just drifting along, as lost as can be.

Current pulls me to shores unknown,
Where fish wear glasses and cows have grown.
I wave to a duck, it quacks in reply,
As I float by on my journey awry.

There's a map, I hear, in someone's hand,
But my GPS says I'm lost in the sand.
I chuckle aloud, what a comedic plot,
Adventures ahead, though the map I forgot.

So here I lie on this river so grand,
With driftwood companions, all singing in band.
We laugh at the weeds picking up our pace,
In this wild, witty wonder, we've found our place.

Moments in the Twilight

Twilight dances on the edge of night,
With jangly laughter and stars shining bright.
I wear my shoes on the wrong feet today,
But who needs a map when you've lost your way?

Chasing shadows that tickle my nose,
While tripping on cobblestones, laughter just flows.
The streetlights wink, they tease as I pass,
Claiming they knew all my secrets and sass.

A jester's cap perched atop my head,
As my feet lead me where the fearless tread.
I stumble through moments, both merry and odd,
Finding joy in the chaos, it's laughter I laud.

The moon serves as my quirky guide,
While jesters and fairies dance side by side.
In this curious twilight where time spins about,
I embrace each blunder, each giggle, each shout.

The Art of Getting Lost

With a flick of my wrist, I toss my plans,
Maps are for those with too many hands.
I roam through fields of confusion and glee,
Rediscovering, oh, what lost can be free!

I once found a cat wearing sunblock and shades,
He said, "Join my club, we're in a parade!"
A raccoon joined in, playing kazoo,
And suddenly life was a wonderful brew.

Turn left, turn right, or even just spin,
Who needs direction when chaos is kin?
With every odd corner, a new laugh awaits,
In the maze of distraction where destiny fais.

So let's raise a toast to wandering feet,
And the magic found in each glorious cheat.
For getting lost is where we belong,
In the art of the fun, where the heart sings its song.

Serendipity in Solitude

Alone in the woods with my socks on the wrong,
The squirrels debate if I'm lost or I'm strong.
A book in my lap that I never did read,
Whispers to me of adventures to heed.

A frog leaps by, and I trip on a root,
In this scene of chaos, my boots stay astute.
With each silly stumble, I find hidden gems,
Secrets of laughter and whimsical stems.

I chat with the trees like they're old pals of mine,
Joking and laughing, sipping on sunshine.
Each laugh echoes softly, a tickle in air,
In solitude's arms, there's a whimsical flair.

So here I sit, with the world swirling 'round,
Finding joy in the quiet, a sweet silly sound.
For in every misstep, serendipity beams,
In the bubble of laughter, I weave all my dreams.

Secrets Beneath the Surface

In depths unknown, I start to roam,
With pockets full of snacks from home.
A compass spins, it seems confused,
Just like my thoughts—totally bruised.

I trip on roots like I'm in a dance,
Each tumble's just my luck and chance.
Trees chuckle softly, they know my plight,
As they stand tall, wise in their height.

Beneath my feet, the mud does squish,
Is this a path or some squishy dish?
In every step, a story's hid,
While I'm just waiting for the trivia bid.

So here's to blunders, mistakes galore,
With each wrong turn, I laugh even more.
For every map I seem to lack,
I find my joy in getting off track.

Horizons Beyond the Visible

I squint at horizons that tease the eye,
Where the sun dips low and clouds float by.
With visions grand but no GPS,
I wander forth, a joyful mess.

Mountains high, they whisper sweet,
'Catch a ride on this road of treats!'
Yet every path I try to take,
Leads me to rest at a giant lake.

Seagulls cackle as I slip and slide,
On rocks so round, I can't abide.
With snacks afloat, a feast awaits,
As I ponder the whims of fateful fates.

Beyond each bend, I hear the call,
Of laughter and joy, I want it all.
For in this grand, confusing dance,
I find life's joy—not just by chance.

The Wanderer's Dilemma

A map rolled up, it fits just right,
But opening it brings sheer fright.
Each route looks like a doodle chart,
Leading me straight to a random park.

The signs they mock, like teasing friends,
'Go left! Go right!' The fun never ends.
But as I search for directions true,
I spot an ice cream truck out of view!

I toss my quest right into the breeze,
And trade directions for a scoop of freeze.
With sprinkles piled high, my laugh's in tow,
I realize my map was wrong—oh no!

Yet who needs routes when the day feels bright?
I'll wander freely, that feels just right.
For every twist may lead to glee,
In this delightful, winding spree.

Whispers of Wayfaring

In every corner, whispers tease,
Of places near and paths that freeze.
I pause to ponder, look around,
And hear the laughter all around.

The squirrels are plotting, I swear it's true,
With acorns gathered for a grand debut.
They scurry off, with purposeful cheer,
While I, lost, just munch on a pear.

A path just vanished, oh dear me so!
Yet nature's charm won't let me go.
Flowers giggle, tickling my toes,
While the breeze whispers secrets nobody knows.

So here I'll roam, without a plan,
With laughter echoing, a happy man.
For every whisper guides my call,
In this grand adventure, I'll have a ball!

Unplanned Adventures

I packed my bags, oh what a sight,
Forgot my snacks, oh what a fright.
With each wrong turn, I found a treat,
Got lost in laughter, this can't be beat.

The GPS said, 'Proceed with care,'
But I took a left — ended up where?
A llama farm? Oh what a score!
Riding llamas, who could ask for more?

My itinerary, a crumpled ball,
Yet every mishap felt like a call.
To dance with fate under the stars,
Counting the blessings, no matter how far.

So here I stand, with my motley crew,
Forget the map, let spontaneity ensue!
Each twist and turn, a story to share,
Unplanned adventures — beyond compare!

The Quest for Purpose

I sought my purpose with grades and charts,
But tripped on shoes that fell apart.
I questioned signs, they all seemed vague,
While searching for answers in a coffee plague.

I joined a class on how to thrive,
But ended up in a dance-off jive.
Purpose found on a neon stage,
When all I wanted was to turn the page.

So here I am, with glowy sticks,
In my quest for truth, I found some kicks.
Chasing goals that rarely align,
Yet smiles and giggles are always divine.

Maybe purpose hides in silly games,
Where laughter leads and joy proclaims.
To dance through doubts, a merry pursuit,
And find what matters in a bumblebee suit!

Compassing My Heart

With compass in hand, I set my course,
But the needle spun like a wild horse.
I followed my gut, took a leap and a dive,
Only to land where the goats connive.

My heart said north, but I went south,
Reverse psychology from my mouth.
Among the trees, I danced with glee,
With squirrels as my witness, a sight to see.

Following feelings instead of the map,
Led me to friendships and a nap.
I ditched the compass, let whimsy steer,
And discovered that joy was always near.

So now I roam with an open heart,
Each day's a riddle, a curious art.
In the chaos, I find the chart,
Navigating joy wherever I start!

Scribbles on the Trail

With a crayon map and a cap on tight,
I set out boldly into the night.
Each scribble a step, a twist and a turn,
As the moonlit path made my worries burn.

Signposts danced, or was it my mind?
"Left or right?" was the question I'd find.
I followed the doodles, tripped on my shoes,
Lost in a forest of whimsical blues.

A trail of giggles led me back home,
Where children play and wild flowers bloom.
I learned from the mishaps, the steps of a fool,
That laughter's the treasure, the ultimate jewel.

Scribbles remind me, each line's filled with cheer,
In the midst of confusion, adventure is near.
So I'll wander on roads, both crooked and straight,
In a world of doodles, I've found my fate!

Trails of the Unsung

I wander with a smile wide,
Maps are drawings tossed aside.
Each turn, a surprise awaits me,
Like lost keys in my coffee spree.

With every twist, I'm led astray,
Like socks that vanish in the fray.
I sketch my path with doodles bright,
A journey boundless, pure delight.

I stop to ask for directions clear,
Only to find that none are near.
The squirrels laugh as I take a chance,
Navigating life's goofy dance.

In this maze, I'll surely roam,
No paper trail to take me home.
But laughter fills the air I breathe,
In the wild unknown, I take my leave.

Forgotten Routes

I took a turn at Billy's spot,
His directions, oh, they mean a lot!
But left and right, I'm all confused,
With every step, my brain's bemused.

The GPS is having fun,
Says 'recalculating,' just begun.
I follow paths where no one goes,
Through bramble weeds and prickly rose.

A signpost says 'Enter at own risk,'
Yet here I am, a brave young brisk.
I'll fashion a route to places grand,
As long as I have snacks in hand.

Who needs a map or a guidebook clear?
I've got my wits and a can of beer!
With every stumble and each wrong track,
The journey's fun, no looking back.

The Art of Getting Lost

In every turn, a chance to play,
I find new paths in a comical way.
With toes all wet from puddles wide,
The world's my stage; I'm joyfully tied.

I tripped on roots and danced on stones,
With laughter ringing like happy tones.
Who needs a plan when chaos reigns?
In every mess, adventure gains!

The map's a myth, a distant fable,
My pants are torn, I'm not quite stable.
Each misstep paves a golden route,
I'll make it home with a wiggle and shout!

So here I go, a champion bold,
With stories of every twist retold.
The art of losing my way so free,
Leads to laughter and a homely glee.

Paradox of the Pilgrim

I set my sights on distant lands,
With a sandwich and no guiding hands.
A compass spins like a whirling top,
And yet I find I'm never lost, just hop.

From city streets to mountain peaks,
Each detour brings the joy it seeks.
I chase the sunset, then the dawn,
With mismatched socks and silly yawn.

The world unfolds in vibrant hues,
Where every wrong turns into a muse.
Maps of folly and quirky lore,
Lead me to laughter, never a bore.

So here I stand, a wanderer proud,
In a tangled crown of a whimsical crowd.
When the seas of confusion start to crash,
I'm the king of chaos, in trouble, I splash!

When Stars Align as Signposts

The stars are all twinkling, so bright,
Yet they don't help much in the night.
I wander with glee, no plan in sight,
Laughing at wrong turns, oh what a fright!

A squirrel directs me, with a wave,
Says right is a shortcut, but it's a rave.
I follow along, feeling quite brave,
In fields full of giggles, I feel like a knave.

The moon has a map, but it's quite whack,
Showing me rivers that seem to lack.
I splashed in the puddles, with courage to stack,
Wishing for guidance, but grace is what I lack.

Yet forward I trudge, through muck and mire,
With laughter as fuel, and joy as my fire.
Who needs a map when the fun's in the choir?
In the dance of the lost, I'm feeling inspired!

Embracing the Unmapped

With a grin, I toss the compass away,
Maps are for rovers who plan every stay.
I tumble through bushes, in wild disarray,
Finding treasure in chaos, come what may.

A bird's eye view shows me missing roads,
I'm just a short walk from where laughter explodes.
Between mishaps and giggles, my spirit loads,
In this playful pandemonium, joy erodes.

Friends join the frolic, with snacks in hand,
We feast on mishaps, it's oh so grand!
Each detour a feast, on whimsy we stand,
In the absence of structure, adventure is planned.

So here we go on this wacky ride,
With no map in hand, but joy as our guide.
Embracing the wild has become our pride,
In laughter we revel, side by side!

The Cartographer's Folly

The map maker chuckled, with ink in his eye,
Claiming to chart where dreams dare to fly.
Yet every fine detail was penned on the sly,
Leading to places that make you ask why.

"I swear it's right there!" he insisted with glee,
As we found ourselves lost, counting one, two, three.
A path lined with donuts had us in spree,
Now we roam for confections, not where we should be.

We searched for the north, but found spinning chairs,
Played hopscotch with turtles and swung in the air.
If laughter's a map, we've traveled in pairs,
To places uncharted, with absolutely no cares.

So let's toast to folly, to wild directions,
To paths full of humor, and sweet imperfections.
For this merry adventure, in silly connections,
Is far more rewarding than perfect reflections!

Fragments of a Lost Map

Crumbled corners hint at where I might go,
Yet the points have faded in a whimsical flow.
With each step I take, more laughter will grow,
As I follow the breadcrumbs, through high and low.

Once I found a marker that said 'You are here,'
But it led to a pond filled with ducks and some beer.
I laughed with the quackers, dropped all my fear,
In this cartwheel of chaos, pure fun is near.

The map now is mere bits of paper and dreams,
Lost in my pocket, it threads through my seams.
I hop like a rabbit, or so it seems,
Chasing the sunlight and skipping the beams.

So here's to the fragments, the jigsaw we share,
To wandering whims and no burdens to bear.
In the landscape of folly, I'm light as the air,
Finding joy in each step, with laughter everywhere!

Wind and Wonder on the Trail

With each step I take, I just guess the way,
A wrong turn here might brighten my day.
The wind in my hair, oh what a fun ride,
Why follow the signs when I can just glide?

I chatted with squirrels, got lost in their chat,
They spoke of the map, but I don't need that!
A bridge made of branches, a stream made of cheer,
I'm tangled in laughter, oh how I steer!

My shoes full of mud, what a stylish trend,
In this wild, wacky world, I surely pretend.
The sun's setting low, in hues bright and bold,
What will tomorrow's mishap unfold?

So here I will dance, with fate as my guide,
Through bushes and thickets, I really won't hide.
Just pull up a chair to this whimsical map,
Let's toast to the fun of this glorious nap!

Aimless Stars in the Sky

Above, the stars twinkle like lost, shiny toys,
Each one a reminder of all my lost joys.
No compass in hand, just a laugh and a grin,
Is it north or is south where the fun might begin?

I gaze at the moon, who seems so confused,
Winking and blinking, he can't be excused.
A constellation of ducks, oh what a sight!
I'll follow what giggles, they steer me just right.

With clouds as my pillows, I drift and I dream,
Chasing those comets, or so it would seem.
Each wish built on starlight, so wobbly yet bright,
I'm like a lost puppy, just out for a bite!

So here's to the misfits, lost in the night,
Let's dance with the moon and embrace the odd light.
For maps are mere pages that point out the past,
I'll wander forever, and have such a blast!

The Longing for Home

With crumbs in my pocket and dreams in my head,
    I wander these roads that twist like a thread.
    I miss my own couch, it's where I belong,
    But adventure's a siren, singing me along.

    A bed made of clouds, oh what a fine jest,
    And donuts with rainbows, I stop for a rest.
    I long for my kitchen with smells that are sweet,
    But I trip on a pickle and laugh at my feet.

    Each twist in this path is a tale yet untold,
With sock-stealing monsters and treasures of gold.
    I stumble on treasures more tasty than pie,
    Yet long for the safety of home's cozy sigh.

So here's to the road less traveled, my friend,
    For I chase after whims that never will end.
    With giggles and grins, let's frolic and roam,
    For inside this chaos, I'm never alone!

When Directions Fade

A GPS voice that I just can't ignore,
Keeps saying 'recalculating'—I'm lost for sure!
The signposts all vanished, disappeared with a wink,
Maybe right's left, or is it that I think?

With each turn I take, I chuckle and wheeze,
My path is a puzzle, a hop, skip, and tease.
The trees are my allies, the bushes my crew,
In a world full of 'where's', I'll find my own view.

Should I follow the butterflies, or dance with the bees?
Every step is a giggle, it's all meant to please.
With crayons for maps, I'll scribble and dash,
My treasure awaits, it's a colorful stash!

So here's to the wanderers, the misfits, the bold,
In this funny old circus, I'm making pure gold.
When directions will fade, I won't shed a tear,
For serendipity, darling, is why I am here!

Navigating the Labyrinth

In this maze of twists and turns,
I trip on shoes, my balance burns.
With a smile, I shout, 'Which way now?'
The compass spins, but I don't know how.

Maps are myths and signs are lost,
I dodge a pond, at what a cost!
Laughter echoes with every step,
Tangled up in paths I inept.

Round and round, I roam in cheer,
As ducks join in, they quack and jeer.
A path to joy, or so they claim,
I just wanted to reach my game!

Through hedges high and bushes wide,
I venture forth, my heart, my guide.
Each wrong turn leads to a new joke,
With every stumble, I laugh and poke.

Directions in Disarray

With a crumpled map and a clueless grin,
I analyze roads, where to begin?
A dog barks loudly, wagging its tail,
Hints of adventure hidden in each trail.

I ask the trees, they whisper vague,
"Just follow the breeze!"—they seem to brag.
Check my watch, but time laughs back,
I'm late again, my plans on a rack.

Street signs dance in a merry waltz,
I point the wrong way, it's all my faults.
Cafés beckon with a tempting treats,
Guess I'll stop here and rest my feet.

With every step, I find new delights,
Random encounters on lonely nights.
Life's signposts wobble, sometimes absurd,
Maybe I'll just follow the song of a bird.

The Journey's Endless Question

Eggshells crack under my carefree feet,
Questions swirl—where's my seat?
A sign says 'Left,' but I'm drawn to right,
Is it a path or just out of sight?

Every turn brings laughter near,
A squirrel's antics, a friendly deer.
'Excuse me, sir, which way to fun?'
With a shrug, he munches—wander on, hon!

The map in hand keeps teasing me,
Reveals a way to foolish glee.
With each wrong twist, my joy expands,
Lost in wonder, I clench my hands.

Is this a trip or a comic play?
With blooms and blooms, come what may.
As questions linger, I leap and soar,
With every misstep, I'm wanting more!

Shadows on the Path

Strolling alongside silly shadows,
They morph and dance like circus glows.
I greet my friends—oh wait, it's grass,
No one here but me to pass.

Twinkling stars start to giggle bright,
"Why not just wander, it feels so right?"
I trip on roots, embrace the ground,
With earthworms joining, friends abound!

Where's the end? Who needs a prize?
The journey's silly with wide-open skies.
Each bend, each hill, sparks joy anew,
As lighthearted moments help me through.

So here I am, navigating mad,
With quirky roads, I can't grow sad.
For silly shadows, foggy nights,
Bring laughter golden, endless delights.

Horizons Beyond Control

I took a turn without a plan,
The GPS is just a fan.
With snacks piled high and coffee strong,
I wave goodbye to where I belong.

The sunset melts with every twist,
Do I drive on or just persist?
The only map I seem to trace,
Is the coffee rings on my face.

Winding roads with no retreat,
A cow observes, I raise a fleet.
With laughter echoing in the air,
I'm lost, but boy, do I not care!

So here I roam, a king unwound,
In this confusion, joy I found.
With every mile and silly plot,
Adventures bloom in every spot.

In Search of Unfamiliar Shores

I packed my bags and left with flair,
But where's the sand? Just fields of air.
The ocean calls, or so I thought,
I'm here with cows, what have I sought?

The waves are just a buzzing sound,
I might need a boat, or just a hound.
Surfboards sit, neglected, dry,
Maybe it's time to just fly high.

With flip-flops on in muddy lanes,
I dance with puddles, who needs chains?
A seagull loops, I wave in jest,
Who needs those shores? I'm on a quest!

Yet the search for shores brings giggles near,
From lost horizons, my path is clear.
So here I Stand, an explorer bold,
With tales of mud instead of gold.

The Enigma of Arrival

Rivers of traffic, I creep and crawl,
A welcome sign? Nah, that's just a mall.
I seek the spot where dreams collide,
But all I find is a teenage ride.

The end of the line, they say with glee,
Yet here I am, lost as can be.
With every corner, a mystery brews,
Did I miss my fate amid mixed views?

Maps betray me with every turn,
But oh, the lessons, happy and stern.
If arriving means standing in line,
I'll thrive on chaos, that suits me fine!

So celebrate mishaps and curious quests,
In every delay, I see the best.
For what's a journey without a bumble?
With laughter aboard, I joyfully tumble!

Searching for Signposts

With eyes peeled wide for signs so clear,
I'm lost between laughter and a sneer.
This road's a mystery, oh what a game,
I'm navigating it, but it's all the same.

The signs lead me to nowhere fast,
A detour here, a question is cast.
Do I turn left or right, who can say?
Maybe I'll wander and call it a day.

Map or no map, I'd still beg to differ,
For life's a film, and I'm the snicker.
With every twist, and puddle to jump,
The journey's the pizza, the map's just the lump!

I chuckle and cheer as I roam around,
For every lost highway, adventure is found.
In search of signposts, I craft my new fate,
With silly detours that I celebrate!

Forks in the Road

Two paths ahead, which one to take?
I'd flip a coin, but it's in the lake!
One's paved with gold, the other with mud,
Guess I'll just follow the sound of the thud.

With every turn, I chase my own tail,
That left was right, but right went pale.
I'll take a selfie at each excursion,
My GPS broke—what a wild version!

A squirrel just waved, I think we're pals,
He points the way, "Just follow the gales!"
But winds are laughing, they won't be tamed,
Anyway, who knew roads could be framed?

So here I am, in a dance with fate,
With half a snack and no dinner date.
Caution to the winds—I'll sing my song,
With every footstep, I can't go wrong!

Secrets in the Side Streets

Wander out past the busy main lane,
Side streets hold secrets, some sweet, some plain.
A cat with a hat and a dog on a swing,
What mischief we'll find, oh, what joy it'll bring!

An alleyway whispers, 'Here's where we play!'
A jazz band is jamming—oh, what a display!
I'll join the conga line, just watch my step,
Tripped on a shoe, now I'm a new rep!

The corners are chuckling, the lampposts grinning,
Turns out this chaos is just the beginning.
Each step leads to laughter, a tale that I'll keep,
In the side streets of chance, far from the deep!

So let's toast to the unknown, mischief's delight,
With garlands of giggles, I'll dance through the night.
No need for a compass, nor map in my hand,
With curious hearts, we parade through this land!

The Road Less Known

I took the road, no one would dare,
With hedges that scratch and branches that snare.
Where is this leading? No clue to unfold,
A sign says 'Welcome' but turns out it's old.

There's a signpost that wobbles, all crooked and bent,
With arrows to places not quite heaven-sent.
Naughty little gnomes are giggling in glee,
Offering cookies if you find the right tree!

Shimmied past boulders, I slip and I slide,
Chasing the whispers that turn like the tide.
No worries, no plans, just curious minds,
What once was a mystery now simply unwinds.

So here's to the path that no one would seek,
With puddles and rainbows, it's never too bleak.
The road less known is my favorite dance,
With laughter and whimsy, I'll take any chance!

Serendipity's Path

Down Serendipity Street, where luck often strays,
I twirled like a leaf in the sun's warm rays.
Found a treasure, a sock, and a half-eaten pie,
Just your average day, oh me, oh my!

A busker was playing, but the tune was upside down,
With every note, I spun in my crown.
I saw a parade of unruly ants,
They marched with such flair, in their tiny pants!

Each step I took, I stumbled on cheer,
The strangers all smiled as I twirled without fear.
A puppy paraded with a ribbon so bright,
My map may be missing, but I'm feeling alright!

So here's to the joy that the random can yield,
When maps are discarded, pure magic is revealed.
Embrace the detours that lead to the flight,
For in the fun chaos, everything feels right!

Echoes of the Wandering Soul

I set out with a plan in mind,
But the road signs weren't all that kind.
Turns I made, both left and right,
Now I'm lost, but what a sight!

With coffee spills and crumbs galore,
I've traveled seas, and oh, much more!
Each laugh a curve, each sneeze a drift,
In chaos, I find my greatest gift.

Maps are dull; they crinkle and fade,
But wandering wild? That's an escapade!
With every wrong turn, I dance and twirl,
In this grand maze, I'm the lost pearl.

So here I roam, without a clue,
Chasing sunsets that paint the blue.
A joyful mess, I'll face the day,
For getting lost is my own ballet.

The Lost Cartographer

With graph paper and pencil in tow,
I set out to chart what I didn't know.
But oops! My lines make a tangled mess,
Winding through trees, I must confess.

I thought I'd trace a path so fine,
Instead, I found a grapevine shrine.
Peculiar sights and cheeky birds,
More plot twists than in a book of words.

My compass spins like a whirling top,
While I'm just trying to find a shop.
Navigating chaos, oh what a prank,
Wandering's fun; who needs to bank?

In every wrong turn, a giggle hides,
Through hills and valleys, my spirit glides.
So here I roam, with no way back,
Cartographer lost, but on the right track!

Unfolding Landscapes

I packed my bags in a fevered rush,
Ready to conquer, oh what a hush!
But unfolded maps were dreaming wide,
Turning around on this crazy ride.

Mountains that looked like giant pies,
Fields of daisies that touch the skies.
Every step leads to quirky tales,
Where squirrels plot and the laughter fails.

Excuse me, sir! Where's the nearest lake?
He points to clouds, for goodness' sake!
But in this puzzle of twist and bend,
I find laughter that has no end.

So onward I prance, with joy unfurled,
Through the absurdities this map has hurled.
In landscapes wild, where whimsy reigns,
I hear the echoes of blessed gains.

Whispers of the Wandering Wind

I hear the breeze fairies plot and scheme,
Guiding the lost on a whimsical dream.
But alas! They laugh as I lose the way,
With jumbled directions that stray and sway.

Through cities bustling and quiet lanes,
I dodge the norms and hitch the trains.
With fridge magnets marking my flights,
I collect mishaps as my guiding lights.

The clouds above, oh, what a delight!
They shift and dance in the fading light.
"Turn left!" they whisper, "or was that right?"
With every gust, I embrace the flight.

So here's to winds and their playful charms,
To getting lost and all of its harms.
Embracing the chaos, come what may,
For in this breeze, I'll find my way.

Sketching New Horizons

With crayons in hand, I draw my way,
Each squiggle a dream, bold and gray.
The lines go wild, not quite straight,
Maybe I'll find that shiny gate.

I scribble the sun, and clouds too,
Mixing colors like a painter's brew.
But what's this path? It leads to a tree,
Where birds throw bananas just for me!

A carrot-shaped car zooms past so fast,
I hop on board, embracing the blast.
Navigating puddles with giggles and cheer,
Who needs a map when smiles are near?

Each twist and turn makes me dance with glee,
Forgotten routes, but I'm still carefree.
In a maze of fun, I totally slip,
Laughing out loud, I embrace the trip!

Labyrinth of Lost Dreams

Stumbling through halls made of my thoughts,
Wandering 'round with tangled knots.
A door swings open, but it leads to a cat,
Who offers me snacks and a funny hat!

I see all my goals in picture frames,
Except for that one with silly names.
Sticky notes glued on a paper wall,
One says, 'Don't forget to stand tall!'

Maps that were drawn in crayon and cheer,
Show paths that vanish, oh dear, oh dear!
I trip on a shoe, that's not even mine,
But I roll with the punch; it's really quite fine.

Each misstep's a giggle, each turn's a delight,
In this zany maze, I find my light.
With dreams that wander, like me they roam,
In the labyrinth of laughs, I always feel home!

Stories Written in Dust

In the attic of memories, I find a chair,
Dust bunnies dance, with wigs in their hair.
Each grain's a story I once forgot,
Of wild adventures I definitely sought.

The dust tells of journeys on bicycles bright,
Chasing after stars late into the night.
A relic of laughter, it starts to twirl,
As moments in time begin to unfurl.

A feathered friend leads the way outdoors,
We scribble our tales beneath the high shores.
With each little step, I humorously scoff,
Who needs a map when we can just laugh?

Skinny dipping in puddles and running from bees,
Stories transforming into delicious memories.
In this dusty vault, with giggles so vast,
It's clear that the fun is what's meant to last!

Secrets of the Open Road

The road is a ribbon of goofy surprise,
With lollipops growing, oh my, what a prize!
A snail in a tux offers a ride,
With hiccups of joy, I hop in with pride.

Billboards that wink and sing silly songs,
Encourage my feet to dance along.
In a car made of marshmallows, we float,
Past cakes and cookies, on a gummy boat!

Each mile unspools like a candy cane's twist,
As I chase down the whims I can't resist.
The license plate reads, 'Crazy But Free,'
Why measure the journey when you're just meant to be?

Laughter erupts like a colorful flare,
In this road trip of dreams, with nary a care.
The secrets unfold with each turn I take,
In the joy of the ride, there's so much to make!

Myriad Ways to Wander

I set out to roam and play,
With sneakers untied, I lost my way.
In circles I twirl, like a lost balloon,
The sun's my compass, or so I assume.

My friends all say I'm quite the guide,
But really I'm just hoping to slide.
Through bushes and trees, I make my own path,
Ha! Found a deer, now doing the math.

I questioned a squirrel, he shrugged and ran,
Can't ask the flowers, they just bloom and tan.
With laughter and snacks, I make my own fun,
And dress up like a tourist, just for the pun!

So here's to the detours, the wrong turns I take,
Each trip's a new tale, a frolic to make.
Forget the map, it's just too boring,
I'll dive headfirst; who knows what's in store-ing?

The Thread of the Unmapped

I strayed from the path, oh what a surprise,
With only my wit and some puzzled eyes.
My shoes got muddy in the muck and the mire,
Yet my sense of adventure is what I admire.

I stumbled on llamas, they looked rather chic,
I asked them for directions, they just gave me a squeak.
I waved bye-bye to logic, it left with my rhyme,
I thought, "Hey, let's just follow this line!"

The trees had opinions, the clouds paced around,
They spoke in riddles, no answers were found.
With wild imaginations, we danced in the breeze,
While the GPS laughed, enjoying the tease.

In this grand confusion, joy is my map,
With a spirit so quirky, maybe I'll nap.
For every lost moment, there's laughter to find,
Let's wander forever, with a whimsical mind!

Amidst the Unknown Terrain

In fields of confusion, I trip and I fall,
With pinecones and rabbits, I seem to enthrall.
An invitation to chaos out here in the wild,
I'm a bumbling explorer, but just like a child.

The rocks begin plotting a hike of their own,
They giggle and shimmer, I feel so alone.
I'll stop for a tea and a chat with a tree,
While squirrels hold court, and the birds disagree.

A path appears layered with leaves and with light,
I pause for a snack and savor the bite.
With every odd corner, I discover a treat,
Like laughter and sunlight, oh, life is so sweet!

So off I shall wander, the bright day ahead,
With nonsense my guide and joy's threads to spread.
I may be off-track, but I surely don't care,
In this fabulous mess, there's adventure to share!

Musings on the Misdirection

I packed my ideas, my snacks, and my hat,
But forgot that travel could make me a brat.
I thought I could dazzle the world with my flair,
Yet I tangled my shoelace, and oh! What a scare!

With every wrong turn, I discover some laughs,
Like stepping on jelly, or dodging giraffes.
The universe chuckles while I make a fuss,
And ends up showing me life's joyous plus.

Exploring without a clue is quite the delight,
I chase after butterflies, they take to flight.
In moments of silliness, I tumble and sway,
There's humor in finding I'm lost on the way.

So let's raise a toast to the paths yet unknown,
To the mishaps and giggles, and seeds we have sown.
For every mishap, there's joy to detect,
In whimsical journeys, we find our own effect!

The Detours We Embrace

I left my house in such a rush,
With just my keys, no time to hush.
Thought I knew the route so well,
But ended up by a taco shell.

The GPS said, "Go left, not right!"
But I took a chance, oh what a sight!
Ended up in a petting zoo,
Who knew llamas were my next view?

I wandered through the streets so wide,
With no direction, just my pride.
Followed a squirrel, thought it was fate,
Now I'm meeting friends at the dinner plate.

Each wrong turn became a thrill,
Mixing up the plan with will.
When I finally get home at night,
I'll laugh at those detours, what a delight!

Wandering Without a Guide

I woke up late with coffee in hand,
No map in sight, just a kid's band.
"Let's see where the wind takes me!"
But I lost my way near a giant tree.

I asked a pigeon for directions,
It cooed back, causing complications.
With no clue how to proceed,
I followed a dog, yes indeed!

Traffic lights were my best friend,
Red meant stop, but oh, I'd bend.
Running in circles, oh such a laugh,
Each wrong turn was a new paragraph.

Wandering freely, laughing out loud,
Embracing the fun amidst the crowd.
A sign that read, "You are quite lost!"
But the smiles I gained covered the cost!

In Search of the Unseen

With a sandwich in one hand, I roamed,
Through places I never called home.
Where am I going? Beats me, dear,
Just following scents, nothing to fear!

An ice cream truck? What a bizarre find,
I chased it down, leaving the grind.
Strangers laughed, called me the parade,
I didn't mind! Sweet treats I made!

Lost in a maze of bright surprise,
With forty cats and a squirrel that flies.
Each corner turned held a new twist,
Like finding treasure in a foggy mist.

What's that on the horizon, oh joy?
A festival? A cute toy?
In search of unseen, my mission's complete,
With memories forged and spontaneous sweet!

Maze of Memories

Woke up in a maze, where to go?
Chasing echoes of my own shadow.
Every pathway has jokes concealed,
A treasure map that's never revealed.

I tried to retrace my steps in vain,
Each wrong turn brought more laughter than pain.
Found a clip-on tie and a bright pink shoe,
In this maze of memories, what a view!

Puns and poodles danced in the street,
Craving adventure, something sweet.
With every twist, a chuckle, a grin,
Embracing the mess, I felt like I'd win.

The walls whispered stories, laughter unbound,
In this crazy labyrinth, joy is found.
So here's to forgetting the map that I had,
For through detours and gaffles, I'm simply glad!

The Wayward Traveler

I set out with a coffee and a dream,
But forgot my GPS, or so it would seem.
I turned left where I should've gone right,
Now I'm lost in a field, oh what a sight!

With a map from the gas station, I squint and muse,
'Cause the only thing clear is the road I refuse.
I follow a cow who seems quite astute,
But he just looks back, chewing grass, how cute!

I asked a kind stranger which way I should roam,
He pointed to nowhere and said, "Just go home!"
I laugh at the chaos, embrace the wrong turn,
Every bump in the road is a lesson to learn!

So here's to the trips that go off the rails,
To the whimsical paths and the map-less trails!
With a grin, I will wander, with no need to flee,
For the best parts of life are wild and free!

Destined to Drift

Woke up with a purpose, but then lost my way,
My compass is spinning—what more can I say?
I've wandered in circles, found a few bright quirks,
Like the goldfish I met, who gave me some smirks!

They say trust the process, it'll all work out fine,
But my process resembles a jumbled design.
With my bag full of snacks and my shoes untied,
I'll follow the sun with a spring in my stride!

Maps and brochures? Nah, I'd rather explore,
Like a kid on a treasure hunt, what's behind that door?
I may drift like a leaf in the wind without care,
But each twist and a turn brings me stories to share!

Oh, the friendships I've found, on this wild spree,
With folks who can laugh at their own mischief, you see.
So cheers to the meanderers and mismatched trails,
For the joy of the journey far outlasts the details!

Where Are We Going?

With a bag full of snacks and a thirst for the views,
I hop in my car, 'what more could I lose?'
The radio's blaring, my playlist's a mess,
I brace for adventure, oh, what a fun stress!

Maps stuck to the seats, I toss them away,
As Google says calm down, "We'll find our own way."
But my phone just ran out—what a twist in the tale,
Now I'm flying with fluffy clouds and dreaming of ale!

I stop for directions, they look at me strange,
They say, "It's around here, or perhaps down the range."
I point to the sky while they point at the floor,
Man, how do you navigate without a store?

So here I am lost, embracing the ride,
Making memories, with laughter as my guide.
With no destination, just fun on repeat,
I'll find my own path, with much more to meet!

A Map of Memories

Who needs a roadmap when you've got a tale?
Each pit stop's a treasure, with laughs to regale.
From epic wrong turns to the snacks that I crave,
Every twist of the route makes my spirit brave!

A diner in nowhere with the best pie in town,
A man on a horseback who wore a wild crown.
With stories to capture as I roam and I sway,
It's these little moments that brighten my day!

The maps fade away, but the smiles stay bright,
With every blunder, I discover new sights.
Through valleys and mountains, oh, what a dance!
In this expedition, I'm given a chance!

So if you lose your way, don't you fret or pout,
Each lost opportunity holds laughter throughout.
For the map of my heart is forever well-trod,
In the funny little journey, I owe it my nod!

Pathways Uncharted

I wandered down a road so wide,
With no clue where I would slide.
A squirrel stopped me, quite a sight,
He pointed left, said 'Go where it's light!'

My shoes are worn from all the trips,
Through puddles deep and donut dips.
I chased a cat, it ran away,
Guess I'm lost, but what a day!

The signs were vague, my phone's a joke,
It directed me to a pile of smoke.
But laughter finds me, keeps my spirits high,
In this big maze, I still can fly!

So here I go, with snacks in hand,
Forget the map, it's a fun-filled land.
With every twist, I feel the cheer,
Who needs directions when laughter's near?

Lost in the Wilderness of Time

Tick-tock, the clock gives chase,
I sprint ahead, but lose my place.
Dandelions dance, they mock my plight,
'Come join us now, forget your fight!'

A step to the left, a twist to the right,
I tripped on a root, oh what a sight!
Time flies in circles, it seems so mean,
Yet frogs serenade, oh what a scene!

Stuck in a loop, the same old joke,
A wise old turtle? Nope, just smoke.
But in this chaos, a grin will spread,
Lost in time, with dreams instead.

So here I stand, with spaghetti hair,
Counting the clouds like counting despair.
With heart in hand, I roam the grind,
The past's a giggle, and I'm feeling fine!

Compass of the Heart

My compass spins, oh what a tease,
It points to pizza? That's sure to please!
With each direction, I lose my way,
But who can complain when you've got Play?

The North says 'scoot', the South says 'stop!',
I chase a rainbow, then stumble and flop.
In search of treasures, I found a shoe,
A single one, but it's good as new!

With giggles and crumbs tucked away in pockets,
Off I go, like some wild rocket!
No maps on this ride, just laughter and cheer,
In the heart's true compass, adventure is near.

So let the wind guide, let the stars align,
With every misstep, I find the divine.
This wild little ride is a glorious art,
Why follow a path? Just trust your heart!

Navigating the Unknown

With a wink and a grin, I set off today,
To navigate the wild, in my special way.
A map? Who needs it? Not this brave soul,
I'll follow the giggles, that's my goal!

Through jungles of socks and forests of cheese,
I'll topple and tumble with elegant ease.
The ground is a trampoline, the trees are a stage,
In this circus of life, I turn the next page!

So many detours, so little regret,
Got lost in a cupcake, maybe a pet!
If laughter is gold, then I'm rich indeed,
In this uncharted path, I've planted a seed.

With friends by my side, we'll conquer the day,
No need for a map: we'll just laugh and play.
Through all of the madness, I rise and I roam,
In the unknown, my heart finds its home!

The Vagabond's Lament

I set out with great flair,
A compass that was broken,
My map blown to the air,
I laughed at the unspoken.

The roads all twist and turn,
Each sign seems to mislead,
With every lesson learned,
I find what I don't need.

I asked a squirrel for tips,
He just twitched his tiny tail,
With no directions in flips,
I wobbled on my trail.

But still I dance and twirl,
Through fields of wild delight,
With no end in this whirl,
I'm lost, but that's alright!

Embracing the Unscripted

I packed my dreams in a sack,
Said goodbye to the map,
With snacks I found in a crack,
And wandered into a flap.

Each corner holds surprise,
Like socks that don't even match,
I grin as I realize,
I've set myself a new catch!

The bus never comes on time,
My sandwich was turned to goo,
Yet laughter is my prime,
As I splatter my shoe.

So here's to the unknown,
With hiccups along the way,
From mishaps brightly shone,
I'll dance until the gray!

The Infinite Road Ahead

The road stretches far and wide,
My GPS took a snooze,
With no guide to be my pride,
I'm free to wander and cruise.

Each mile brings a fresh surprise,
From puddles that sing and splash,
I search for my lost prize,
A map? Well, that's just brash!

I met a cow with wise eyes,
She mooed in philosophical tones,
Her wisdom? Just some good fries,
And a barn full of funny moans.

So I march on with glee,
Each step a silly dance,
Who needs plans, not me,
I'm in the absurd chance!

The Heart's Wilderness

My heart is a thicket wild,
Where pathways weave and wind,
No straight lines, just smiles mild,
And joy from what I find.

A bird offered to show me,
How to find my way around,
But I laughed, thinking of free,
As I tumbled to the ground!

With every branch a misstep,
And bushes that hug me tight,
I've learned to dance and prep,
To sway with whimsy day and night.

So here I roam untamed,
In this bewildered expanse,
Clueless but unashamed,
I turn each thrill to chance!

Where Footprints Vanish

I set out with shoes all shiny,
Planned each step but was quite whiny.
The path turned muddy, oh what a mess,
Now my feet's a colorful dress.

Maps in my pocket, I thought I was slick,
Until I found I had chosen the wrong pick.
Now I'm in circles, feels like a game,
But laughing at chaos, oh what a claim!

Should've asked directions from a passing cat,
Instead of my GPS, that's a fact!
It told me to drive, but I took a stroll,
And here I am, losing all control.

Yet in the snags, there's joy anew,
Each twist and turn, old friends that grew.
For no map's needed when joy's the way,
Laughing and learning as I sway.

A Canvas for the Unsure

I set out with colors in my hands,
To paint my path across the lands.
But every brush stroke turned into a splat,
Creating a canvas of a haphazard chat.

Blues turned to yellows, reds met with green,
What was the picture? No clue, never seen!
With each mishap, I giggled with glee,
For in every flunk, there's beauty—you see!

Turn left at the tree, oh wait, that's a bush,
Now I'm stuck in a clump of shush-shush!
But I wave it off with a wink and a grin,
No perfect ending, let the fun begin!

Each detour a stroke on my canvas bright,
With nobody's rules to restrict my flight.
So here's to the chaos, the giggles we share,
In the gallery of life, we can paint anywhere!

Treasures in the Twists

The road took twists like a curly fry,
I'm lost in laughter, oh me, oh my!
Turned a corner, bumped into a fence,
Found a hedgehog with a look so intense.

Every misstep has a treasure in tow,
Stumbled on noodles, who knew they could flow?
With forks and noodles dancing in place,
Turns out I'm in a spaghetto race!

I thought I'd planned for a stroll through the park,
But ended up on a riverboat in the dark.
The captain just winked, said, "Welcome aboard!"
Now every splash is a laughter-stored hoard!

Beneath every blunder, a gem can be found,
Turn your frown upside down; spin all around!
For the finest treasures are usually concealed,
In the clever mishaps life has revealed.

Finding Joy in Misdirection

I packed my bags and set sail for fun,
With a map that was drawn by a dog on the run.
Every arrow points to colorful chaos,
Yet here I am, caught in a delphos!

Right at the fork? No, let's take the left!
Stumbled on a yard sale; found time's theft.
Haggling over knick-knacks, I lost track of time,
But who needs a schedule when life feels sublime?

And oh! What's that? A llama in shades?
Wandering with flair, as my confusion cascades.
We paused for a selfie, both clueless but cool,
In the art of missteps, we'll make our own rule.

So here's to the turns that don't lead us astray,
With laughter our compass, we'll find our own way.
For in every misdirection, a giggle awaits,
Embrace all the blunders, oh, aren't they just great?

The Detours of Destiny

I packed my bags with glee,
But turned left when I should've turned tree.
The GPS said, "Recalculating,"
While I just stood there, contemplating.

My best-laid plans went awry,
Passed by a frog who looked awfully sly.
I waved goodbye to the road well-trod,
And discovered the locals country-clod.

I met a goat who offered me tea,
"Just grab a chair, don't worry," said he.
We laughed about all my missed turns,
While I scribbled down life lessons to learn.

With no destination in sight,
I danced in the rain under pale moonlight.
And when I finally got back on track,
I realized I'd never look back.

Charting the Uncharted

With crayons and a napkin map,
I thought I had everything to trap.
But soon I was lost in a wild bazaar,
Purchasing snacks from a tiny guitar.

The compass spun like a merry-go-round,
As I wandered far from what's normally found.
"Just follow your heart!" a parrot proclaimed,
Too bad it didn't say 'when you're maimed.'

Through conga lines and a juggling clown,
I lost my way through this crazy town.
But every wrong turn felt so right,
As I danced with strangers late into the night.

I charted a course on the fly,
Under a sky with custard pie.
And realized maps are just for the meek,
While laughter and mischief are what we seek.

The Scenic Route Home

I took the scenic route, or so I thought,
Next to a llama who happily fought.
With each twist and turn, I just had to shout,
"Who knew the road had this much clout?"

A sign read 'Beach' but I found a lake,
Where swimmers splashed with an enormous cake.
I dove right in with my clothes still on,
Turns out my journey was far from gone.

The view was great, with sunsets so bright,
I blinked away worries, it felt so right.
Not a soul around to give me a look,
But a turtle popped up with a guidebook.

So here's to detours that lead us to cheer,
To moments of joy that we hold so dear.
Navigating life without a clear road,
Is just another form of adventure, I'm told.

Finding Direction in Chaos

With a map that looked more like a doodle,
I faced the world, ready to poodle.
Every turn led to a cheerful surprise,
Like a monkey wearing sunglasses, oh my, what a prize!

I asked a squirrel for secret advice,
He pointed north, said it's simply nice.
But I ended up lost in a candy shop,
With lollipops raining, I just couldn't stop!

Behind a blue door with glittering lights,
I bumped into folks having feathery fights.
They handed me cupcakes and shareable laughs,
While my map was turned into scraps and half-hafts.

In the chaos, I found my own way,
With giggles and sprinkles guiding the day.
So if you're lost, just don't hit snooze,
Embrace the madness; it's yours to choose.

The Scenic Route of Existence

I wandered down a winding lane,
My GPS lost, it's all in vain.
Bumping into walls of my own design,
Sipped coffee with the sun, feeling fine.

The bus missed its stop, I missed my train,
Lost in thoughts, dancing in rain.
With every turn, a laugh, a smile,
Wondering if I left in style.

An old map tucked, I can't find a clue,
But joy is my compass, it's perfectly true.
Skyscrapers loom like friendly giants,
And robots wave like nostalgic clients.

Paved paths are boring, that's my decree,
Give me a shortcut, with snacks and glee.
In circles I roam, forever a scout,
The scenic detour, I'm not leaving out.

Chronicles of a Wayward Traveler

With mismatched shoes, I hit the street,
Checking maps that refuse to repeat.
Every roadside stand knows me well,
I barter snacks for stories to tell.

A wrong turn leads to a charming café,
Where time slows down and worries give way.
I trip over shoes, an ungraceful dance,
Laughing at fate, it's my second chance.

I've ridden camels, danced with a cat,
Got lost in a maze filled with shiny flat.
In the land of 'Oops,' all's fun and bright,
Every misstep is pure delight.

Traveling light? That's just not my style,
With bags overflowing, I own every mile.
Each broken compass, a tale I'll spin,
In this adventure, I feel the win.

Between Destinations and Dreams

Maps are overrated, I prefer the thrill,
Finding secret spots, and climbing the hill.
Every corner turned reveals a treat,
The quirky café or the funny seat.

Lost in translation, words gone awry,
Strangers become friends as we share a fry.
Navigating life like a blindfolded game,
Yet every wrong turn seems just the same.

In shops and stalls, I barter my woes,
A smile for a trinket, that's how it goes.
Between dreams I wander, catching a breeze,
Life's a circus, I'm juggling with ease.

Too many bags and not enough sense,
Crammed in a car, what's all this suspense?
But laughter is golden, I'll take the leap,
In this chaos, I find dreams to keep.

Unfolding Horizons

Setting off with a burst, not a clue,
Where the road ends, no one quite knew.
In flip-flops and shades, I walked the line,
Getting lost in paradise, feeling divine.

My phone's got no signal, the horizon's a blur,
Finding coconuts, applying sunscreen stir.
Each detour a dance, each stop a delight,
Who knew adventure could be so light?

With snack breaks aplenty, and laughter on loan,
I'm carving my path, without a groan.
Every silly mishap a reason to grin,
In this theater of travel, I'm ready to win.

Chasing sunsets that lead to my bed,
Waking to dreams of the journeys ahead.
So here's to the wanderers, unplanned and free,
In the tale of my travels, come join with me!

The Journey of a Thousand Turns

Off I go, my path unclear,
Dodging trees and wild deer,
Maps are lost, but that's okay,
I'll freestyle my way, come what may.

Every twist, a surprise or two,
Found a taco truck, who knew?
But wait, is this a circle I see?
I'll just grab another nacho and flee!

A signpost stands, but it's all a bluff,
'Turn left here,' it scoffs, 'that's enough!'
With every step, I share a laugh,
These misadventures? My secret path.

So join me, friends, don't be shy,
We'll get lost, oh my, oh my!
With giggles and grumbles, off we prance,
In this silly, twisty, endless dance!

Stitching Together a Tattered Route

Pinches of luck, a dollop of grime,
Stitching this journey, one step at a time.
With shoes that squeak and a sock that slides,
I'm holding my map, but where's the guide?

Fabric of dreams, with threads that fray,
I sew in chaos, come what may.
Each bump in the road, a patch I apply,
Hope it's not my pants that'll say goodbye!

Right turns lead me to lefty lanes,
Avoiding puddles and slippery trains.
A quilt of mishaps, I bravely wear,
Each flap laughs loudly, without a care.

So here's to the seams of the paths we weave,
With stitches of hope, there's much to achieve!
As long as I laugh, I'll take it all in,
Tattered or not, let the adventure begin!

Wandering the Unknown

Wander, wander, my feet take flight,
With shadows dancing, I greet the night.
Every corner, a riddle, a joke,
The moon joins me, no need to provoke.

Open fields and a singing brook,
As I follow my whims, I take a look.
What's that? A gnome! Not part of my plan,
But he winks and shares his secret, 'You can!'

Glorious chaos, a magical mess,
With a map that's more of a wild guess.
I chase after squirrels, I tumble and fall,
Yet every misstep brings joy after all.

So here's my heart in the wild I'll roam,
The unknown feels just like home.
With laughter leading this carefree spree,
Every twist is a chance to just be free!

Lost Without a Compass

A compass? Nah, I tossed it away,
Trusting my instincts to lead the way.
But wait, was that north? Now I'm not sure,
I guess I'll just stroll, that's the allure!

Navigating life on a unicycle tire,
Every swing and sway, a new place to admire.
A detour here and a pitstop there,
Found a cat cafe? I'll stop for a chair!

Every fork in the road gets a chuckle from me,
I wave at the bushes, 'We're wild and free!'
And if I get lost, I'll just chalk it up,
To finding new hiccups, just fill my cup!

So here's to the "wrong" that feels so right,
With laughter lighting my way at night.
I'm lost without clues, but truly, that's fine,
In this misfit adventure, I'll claim what is mine!

www.ingramcontent.com/pod-product-compliance
Lightning Source LLC
Chambersburg PA
CBHW072216070526
44585CB00015B/1356